Special Days

Contents

Written by Marie Gabriel

Introduction

All places have special days,
when we sing, dance,
and have treats.

May Day

May Day is a special day
in England.
It is for the end of winter.
We dance about the maypole.
We sing old songs.

Teachers' Day

Teachers' Day is a special day in Malaysia.
It is for our teachers.
They get flowers.
We sing them songs.

Canada Day

Canada Day is a special day
in Canada.
It is for the day
Canada was born.
We have fireworks and parades.
We sing the special song
of our land.

Spring Festival

China has special days
for Spring Festival.
We have treats and fireworks.
We sing and dance.

Anzac Day

Anzac Day is a special day in Australia and New Zealand. We think about our brave soldiers. We sing the special songs of our lands.

Children's Day

Children's Day is a special day in Japan.
We have kites that look like fish.
We sing a song about the kites.

Index